HISTORIC
COMMUNITIES

Settler Sayings

Bobbie Kalman

Crabtree Publishing Company

www.crabtreebooks.com

HISTORIC
COMMUNITIES

Created by Bobbie Kalman

For Caroline Crabtree

Editor-in-Chief
Bobbie Kalman

Writing team
Bobbie Kalman
David Schimpky
Petrina Gentile
Tammy Everts

Editors
Tammy Everts
David Schimpky
Petrina Gentile
Lynda Hale

Computer design
Lynda Hale

Illustrations
Barb Bedell: cover
Antoinette "Cookie" DeBiasi
Andy Cienik
Tammy Everts
Halina Below-Spada

Color separations
Book Art Inc.

Printer
Worzalla Publishing

Special thanks to
Rose Hasner and the Black Creek Pioneer
Village/TRCA, and the Niagara Apothecary

Published by
Crabtree Publishing Company
www.crabtreebooks.com   1-800-387-7650

PMB 16A   612 Welland Avenue   73 Lime Walk
350 Fifth Avenue, St. Catharines,   Headington,
Suite 3308   Ontario   Oxford
New York, NY   Canada   OX3 7AD
10118   L2M 5V6   United Kingdom

Cataloging in Publication Data
Kalman, Bobbie, 1947-
   Settler sayings

(Historic communities series)
Includes index.
ISBN 0-86505-498-3 (library bound) ISBN 0-86505-518-1 (pbk.)
This book explores the words, phrases, and sayings that were used
by settlers in North America and looks at their modern meanings.

1. Pioneers - North America - Quotations, maxims, etc. - Juvenile
literature. I. Title. II. Series: Kalman, Bobbie, 1947-   . Historic
communities series.

PN6321K3 1994   j428.00973 20   LC 94-5128

Contents

apple-pie order milling about

go off half cocked

mind your Ps and Qs

off by a long shot

Put your nose to
the grindstone!

He bought the farm!

get down to brass tacks

spinster

goose bumps

straitlaced

gone to pot

Don't let the
bedbugs bite

the black sheep

put through the mill

roughed up

lock, stock, and barrel

like a millstone
around your neck

too many irons in the fire

Potluck

I'll be there
with bells on!

I'm stumped

dog days of summer

Show your mettle!

go at it hammer and tongs

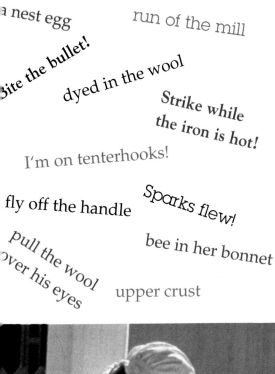

a nest egg   run of the mill

Bite the bullet!

dyed in the wool

Strike while the iron is hot!

I'm on tenterhooks!

fly off the handle   Sparks flew!

Pull the wool over his eyes   bee in her bonnet   upper crust

Say what you mean!

Do adults sometimes say things to you that make absolutely no sense whatsoever? Has your mother ever told you not to count your chickens before they're hatched, for example? You probably gave her a puzzled look and wondered what kind of herbal tea she was drinking!

More than likely, your mother has never counted chickens. She learned the expression from her parents, who learned it from their parents. In fact, before you know it, old sayings will start sneaking into your conversation. When someone invites you to a party, you might just say, "I'll be there with bells on!" and not know why you said it.

Hundreds of years old

Although this book is called *Settler Sayings*, not all the expressions it contains were made up by the settlers; the sayings are very old. The settlers did, however, use them often. The meanings were very clear because the sayings were rooted in situations that occurred in everyday life. When people said "sparks flew," for example, they were comparing an argument to the sparks created when tools were sharpened on a grindstone.

Which iron is that?

Most of us don't think about how old sayings originated. This book explains the source of the sayings as well as how they are used today. The next time someone tells you to "strike while the iron is hot," you will know that he or she is suggesting that you use a good opportunity. You are not being asked to hit someone while your mother or father is ironing a shirt!

In the kitchen

The settlers grew and prepared most of their own food. Many of the words and phrases that people use today came from kitchen sayings of long ago.

Upper crust

Wheat flour was considered better than flour made from other types of grain, and it was often more expensive. Housewives who wished to impress others used the best flour for the upper crust of their pies because it could be seen and admired. The phrase "upper crust" refers to someone or something that is rich or fancy.

This woman is making sure that her dessert is in "apple-pie order." The upper crust of her pie is made with expensive wheat flour because it is the crust that people see. The bottom crust, which is hidden by the pie filling, is made with inexpensive rye flour.

Apple-pie order

When baking an apple pie, settler women made sure they cut the apple slices in equal sizes. The slices were arranged in even rows inside the pie, and the upper and lower crusts were joined with perfectly spaced pinches. "Apple-pie order" describes something that is very tidy.

Cut and dried

The settlers used herbs for food and medicine. They had special gardens in which they grew these herbs. In autumn the herbs were cut, gathered, and hung over the fireplace to dry. When people say that an idea or opinion is "cut and dried," they mean that it has been around for a while and is not likely to change. "Cut and dried" can also mean ordinary or common.

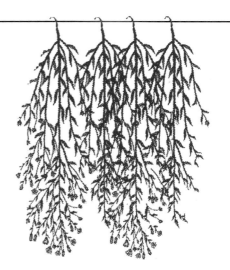

Cut-and-dried herbs could be saved for a long time. In what way are some people's opinions "cut and dried?"

Potluck

If unexpected visitors were invited to dinner, they ate **potluck**, which meant they shared what was in the pot over the fire and hoped for the best. Today a potluck meal can be a meal of leftover foods or a large meal to which all the guests bring food to share. Nobody knows what anyone else is bringing, so a potluck dinner is a surprise for those who eat it!

Gone to pot

Candles were made by dipping a wick repeatedly in candle wax and letting the wax harden. When candles burned low, the leftover pieces were put into a **melting pot** and used to make new candles. The candle pieces had "gone to pot" because they were no longer useful. The saying "gone to pot" refers to something that is beyond repair. It does not mean that someone has gained weight around his or her middle!

What's in the pot tonight? This boy wonders if eating at his friend's house was a good idea.

Spinning and weaving

The settlers had to make their clothes from scratch. Many modern words and sayings came from the tools and methods used to spin yarn, weave cloth, and dye wool.

"She's a spinster!"

Spinning wool into thread was the first step in the cloth-making process. The people who performed this task were called "spinsters." Spinsters were usually the unmarried women in a family. Eventually all unmarried women—whether they could spin or not—were called spinsters. Most women today hate this word!

Shuttle

Weaving is the meshing together of threads that run in different directions. A **shuttle** is a weaving tool that carries the **weft**, or crosswise, threads between the **warp**, or lengthwise, threads on a loom. It is thrown from the left to right and back again. You may hear the word "shuttle" used in "shuttle service," "shuttle bus," or "shuttle train" to describe a transportation system that moves people quickly from one place to another.

To be on tenterhooks

Newly-woven cloth was stretched across **tenter frames** and attached using **tenterhooks**. The stretching kept the fabric from shrinking. Today a person who is in suspense might use the expression that he or she is "on tenterhooks." How can you compare being stretched tightly across a frame to feeling unsure or nervous?

A spinster was a woman who spun wool into thread. "Spinster" later became a name for an unmarried woman. Today unmarried women do not want to be called spinsters!

Fast-moving modern space shuttles are named after this fast-moving early-settler weaving tool.

A heckle, or hackle, was used in making linen. Flax was pulled through its nails to get rid of the broken pieces and tangles. To "heckle" means to tease someone. Perhaps people who are annoyed by others feel as if they are being pulled through a heckle!

This woman is dyeing wool before she spins it into yarn. Sometimes cloth was dyed after it was woven, but fabric that was "dyed in the wool" had longer-lasting color. A stubborn person whose opinions do not change easily is described as "dyed in the wool."

Although the settlers made wool and linen fabric, they bought cotton cloth at the general store. In early general stores, brass tacks were used for measuring lengths of cloth. They were pushed in at regular spaces along the edge of a countertop. Buying cloth could take a long time because the customer and storekeeper usually argued over the price. When the bartering was finally over, they "got down to brass tacks," or measured the cloth. Today people use this saying to mean "getting down to business" or "getting to the point."

On the farm

Many early farming words and sayings have become part of our modern vocabulary. Read the words and sayings on these pages, then turn the page and look for each one in the picture. We hope you are not "stumped!"

Nest egg

Chickens were very important to the survival of the settlers. Farmers used their eggs and meat as food. To encourage hens to lay eggs, farmers placed fake eggs in a hen's nest. Farm children made eggs from clay and painted them with whitewash. Nest eggs were saved and used again when they were needed. Nowadays, a "nest egg" refers to money that is saved for the future.

What do you think "Don't count your chickens before they're hatched" means?

A chicken with its head cut off

When a farmer killed a chicken for food, he or she chopped off its head. For a short time afterward, the chicken's nervous system continued to work and control its movements. Imagine seeing a chicken's body running around without a head! People often use the expression "running around like a chicken with its head cut off" to mean they have so many things on their mind that they don't know what to do first.

Goose bumps

Settlers plucked geese and used their feathers to stuff pillows, mattresses, and bed covers. Like all birds, geese have tiny muscles in their skin that keep them warm. After a goose has its feathers plucked, its skin develops raised bumps. Our skin develops similar bumps. We say we have "goose bumps" or "goose pimples" if our skin gets bumpy when we are cold or afraid.

Apple of one's eye

Have you ever been "the apple of someone's eye?" Long ago, the **pupil**, the black circular center of the eye, was called the apple of the eye. Many people thought the pupil resembled an apple. In Old English, the word *æppel* means "eye" as well as "apple." Today "the apple of one's eye" is someone who is greatly valued or treasured. Can you guess why?

The "dog days" of summer

Today some people believe that the hottest days of summer are called "dog days" because heat can make dogs irritable. The early settlers knew the real secret of this phrase. They kept track of the movements of the stars. They knew that Sirius, the Dog Star, rises with the sun during the hottest time of the year.

Bought the farm

The expression "bought the farm" was used in the military to refer to a soldier who was killed in battle. Many soldiers dreamed of returning home, buying a farm, and settling down. When a soldier died, or "bought the farm," he finally found peace from war. This phrase still means that someone has died, but it is not a very polite way of saying so.

The "black sheep"

Most sheep are white, but sometimes a black sheep is born. These sheep stand out from the others in the herd. Nowadays, a "black sheep" is someone who is different from the rest of his or her family.

In two shakes of a lamb's tail

If you've ever seen a lamb, you know that its tail moves very quickly. When we use the expression "in two shakes of a lamb's tail," we mean "in little or no time at all."

Spuds

The settlers planted all kinds of vegetables. About one hundred years ago, however, people thought potatoes were unhealthy. To discourage people from eating potatoes, a health-conscious group started the Society for the Prevention of Unwholesome Diets. The initials of the group's name formed the word "spud." Today many people refer to potatoes as "spuds."

Small potatoes

Farmers fed small potatoes to their cattle and pigs because these tiny spuds were considered unsuitable for people. Nowadays, "small potatoes" refers to something that is not very important or valuable.

Bees

Honeybees cooperate as they work hard to make honey. Whenever families and friends in a settler community gathered together to work, the event was called a "bee." Settlers held quilting bees, apple-peeling bees, corn-husking bees, and logging bees to get difficult work done quickly. After the work was completed, the settlers celebrated with a party!

"I'm stumped!"

Farmers chopped down trees to clear the land for crops. The stumps of the trees were a nuisance because it was almost impossible to pull them out of the ground. Some farmers tried to dig out the stumps or blast them loose with gunpowder. Others wrapped a chain around the stump and attached the other end to the yoke of an ox. The ox pulled with all its might. "To be stumped" now means to be baffled or confused, which is probably how farmers felt as they tried to budge the stubborn stumps from the ground!

HMMM!?

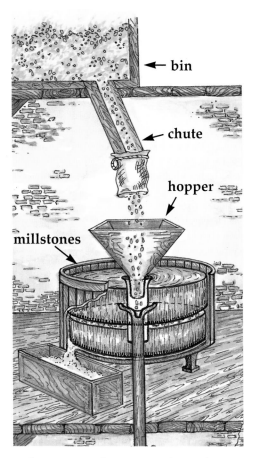

bin

chute

hopper

millstones

When you've been "put through the mill," do you feel as if you've been dropped, spun in circles, and crunched?

The miller used the "rule of thumb" to judge if wheat was properly ground. He rubbed the flour between his thumb and fingers to test its quality. "Rule of thumb" has come to mean the accepted way of doing something.

The miller

In early settler communities, farmers took their grain to the **gristmill** to be ground into flour. The gristmill was an important part of the community. Many sayings came from the tools that were used at the mill and the work that was done there.

Put through the mill

The grain was poured into a large bin on the second or third floor of the mill, fell down a wooden chute, and then passed through a hopper into the center of two large millstones. The millstones rotated in different directions and crushed the grains of wheat between them. A person who is having troubles might say that he or she has been "put through the mill." Why do you think someone might compare experiencing problems to grain going through a mill?

Like a millstone around your neck

The millstone was an enormous, heavy stone. When people have problems that are worrying them, they say that these problems are like "millstones around their necks." How is a problem like a heavy weight?

Roughed up

Millstones had grooves, or **burrows**, on their surface that ripped off the grain's outer husk and directed the ground flour to the outside of the spinning stones. After a few weeks the grooves smoothed out and needed to be "roughed up" or **dressed** again. Today the expression "roughed up" means to be beaten up. Can you explain why?

Show your mettle

Dressing stones could be painful work. As the dresser chipped away at the stone with his millpick, small pieces of stone, as well as metal from the tools, flew through the air and stuck in the back of his hands. The more slivers a dresser had, the more experienced he was. He could "show his mettle" (an old way of spelling "metal") to anyone who asked him how much work he had done. If someone asks you to "show your mettle," they want you to prove your skill, courage, or strength.

Run of the mill

The miller operated, adjusted, and repaired the machinery in the mill. Although running the mill was hard work, it became a routine job for the miller. Today "run of the mill" means plain or ordinary.

*The **dresser** "roughed up" the millstone by chipping away pieces of it to create grooves. Some of the stone chips stuck in the back of his hands.*

*Settlers from near and far traveled to the **gristmill**. People often lined up and waited several hours to have their grain ground. They "milled about" outside and caught up on the village news while they waited for their flour. Nowadays, this expression describes people or animals that move around without a purpose.*

Artisan sayings

Community artisans made all the goods and tools the settlers needed. Many of the sayings that described the work done by these craftspeople are still a part of the language we use.

Irons, hammers, and tongs

The blacksmith used long-handled **tongs** for placing metal in the **forge**. If a blacksmith put "too many irons in the fire" and didn't have a chance to shape them quickly with his hammer, some of the iron could be ruined. Nowadays, the phrase "too many irons in the fire" means that a person is trying to do too many things at once. To "go at it hammer and tongs" means to do something with a lot of energy and enthusiasm.

A **blacksmith** *shaped iron into objects by hammering and bending them. He was known as a "smith" because he would hit or "smite" the hot metal. The first half of the name "blacksmith" originated from the blacksmith's use of iron, which is black. "Sparks flew" when he hit the hot metal.*

Strike while the iron is hot

This popular saying means that a person should take advantage of good opportunities. In settler times the blacksmith heated iron and hammered it into items such as horseshoes or nails. The iron was easiest to bend while it was very hot, just as people are most likely to succeed if they do something when the time is right.

Sparks flew

Have you ever heard someone say that "sparks flew" during an argument? This phrase originated from using a **grindstone** to sharpen tools. When a piece of metal was placed against the turning grindstone, sparks flew.

Fly off the handle

It was very important that the tools used by the settlers were well crafted. If the head of an ax, for example, was not properly attached to its handle, it could fly off when a person was chopping wood. A flying axhead was very dangerous! To "fly off the handle" now means to get upset and lose control of one's temper.

UPPER and lower cases

In settler days the printer printed the village newspaper and advertisements. He or she kept the different type letters, or **sorts**, in four type cases, which were full of tiny storage compartments. The upper two cases held the capital letters; the lower two held the small letters. That is why we refer to capital letters as "UPPER CASE" and regular letters as "lower case." The printer was "out of sorts" if he or she ran out of type letters. Today people are said to be "out of sorts" when they are grumpy.

*As a **grindstone** was turned, the part of the tool that needed sharpening was pressed against the stone. Some tools had to be pressed hard. As a result, the person operating the grindstone had his or her face near the stone. Today "put your nose to the grindstone" means "put more effort into your work."*

The printer kept his or her letters in boxes with small compartments. He or she typeset stories and advertisements one letter at a time!

Inns and travel

Stagecoaches

Horsedrawn carriages called **stagecoaches** were used to carry passengers, mail, or parcels on long journeys. The distance between two stops on a trip was called a "stage" of the journey. That is why the carriages were known as stagecoaches. At each stop the driver changed horses, and the passengers stretched their legs. After the horses were changed, the next stage of the journey began.

In settler times, people depended on horses for travel. Travelers took **stagecoaches** *from town to town and stayed at inns overnight. The following day they began the next "stage" of the journey.*

With bells on!

If wealthy settlers were going to a special event, they put the very best harness on their team of horses. Fancy harnesses were usually equipped with bells. If you say "I'll be there with bells on," you mean you will arrive happy and excited.

harness bells

Mind your Ps and Qs

Inns were merry places where people stayed during their travels or gathered to talk and drink beer and liquor. Mugs of beer could be ordered in two sizes: pints and quarts. If a customer behaved badly, the innkeeper told that person to mind his or her "Ps and Qs," or remember how much he or she had already drunk. Today this phrase means "mind your manners."

This customer looks well behaved. The innkeeper will probably not have to ask him to "mind his Ps and Qs."

Don't let the bedbugs bite

The beds found in homes and inns were very different from the beds of today. The mattresses of the settlers were made of straw, feathers, or a mixture of the two. All kinds of insects lived in these mattresses, resulting in insect bites and sleepless nights for those who slept on the beds! Although today's beds are usually free of insects, we still say "don't let the bedbugs bite" to mean "sleep well."

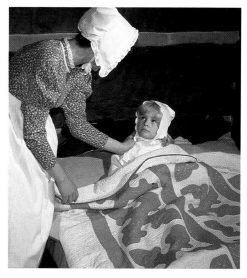

Stogie

Have you ever heard someone call a cigar a **stogie**? In the nineteenth century, many Conestoga-wagon drivers enjoyed smoking strong, cheap cigars. They believed that cigar smoke kept the dust out of their throats. These cigars became known as "Conestogas," or "stogies" for short.

This young girl does not seem eager to go to bed. Perhaps she is worried that the bedbugs will be biting tonight!

The language of fashion

Women who forgot to wear their pattens were considered sloppy or "slipshod."

"Straitlaced" opinions are stiff and unbending, just as corsets were.

Have you ever had the "wool pulled over your eyes?" You might have felt as embarrassed as this man did.

Has someone ever accused you of having a "bee in your bonnet?" Have you ever "pulled the wool over someone's eyes?" Many popular words and phrases came from the words used to describe the fashions and accessories worn in the eighteenth and nineteenth centuries.

Slipshod

Well-dressed women wore dainty shoes made of fabric or thin leather called **slippers**. When it was muddy outdoors, they wore **pattens** to protect their footwear. A patten was a platform set on a metal ring. It was strapped beneath the shoe to raise it above the mud. Only a sloppy woman went outside "slipper-shod" ("slipshod"), or without pattens. Today, if something looks as if it has been done quickly and thoughtlessly, we describe it as "slipshod."

Straitlaced

In the past, fashionable women wore **corsets** that were very tightly laced. The corsets made waists look narrow and kept backs straight. Some corsets were laced so tightly that the women who wore them were hardly able to move or bend. When someone today has strict moral values and "unbending" opinions, we call them "straitlaced."

Pull the wool over his eyes

This phrase goes back to the days when gentlemen wore powdered wigs. Many wigs were made from wool, so "wool" became a popular nickname for a wig. The expression "pull the wool over his eyes" came from the practical joke of tilting a man's wig over his eyes so that he could not see. Today we say that we have "pulled the wool over someone's eyes" when we have fooled or tricked that person.

Denim

"Denim" was the settler way of pronouncing "de Nîmes," which means "of or from Nîmes," a city in France. Hundreds of years ago Nîmes was an important center for the production of textiles. One particular fabric manufactured there was used in making blue jeans. This cloth is still called denim. Some people today refer to their blue jeans as denims.

Denim fabric was once made in a city called Nîmes.

Bee in her bonnet

Settler women often wore bonnets. When a woman removed the bonnet from her head and allowed it to hang down her back by its ties, a bee sometimes landed in it and was trapped. As the woman put the bonnet back on, she had a "bee in her bonnet!" Nowadays, this expression means to be very annoyed by a particular thing.

Having a "bee in one's bonnet" would surely cause a person to be annoyed!

Milliners

The word "milliner" came from the city of Milan in Italy. Milan was a famous fashion center where items such as hats, fine fabrics, and stylish clothes were made for women. "Milaner" was a name for people who lived in Milan. Eventually, the merchants who imported and sold clothes also came to be known as "Milaners" or "milliners." Today a milliner is someone who designs and sells women's hats and accessories.

Milliners imported fancy hats, clothes, and accessories for fashionable settler women.

Guns and ammunition

It was difficult to find a settler family that did not own a gun. Guns were necessary for hunting animals, protecting families, and defending the community. It is no wonder that many sayings came from describing and using guns.

Lock, stock, and barrel

The musket was made up of three main parts: 1. the **lock** ignited the powder, which fired the gun; 2. the **stock** was the wooden part of the gun; 3. the **barrel** was the long tube that held the ball and powder. "Lock, stock, and barrel," which referred to all the parts of a gun, now means "everything." To move "lock, stock, and barrel," for example, means to take everything from one location to another.

Flash in the pan

In settler days loading a gun called a **musket** was a complicated task. The **pan** was the part of the gun that was filled with a small amount of gunpowder. A tiny hole connected the powder in the pan to the powder inside the gun. When the musket was fired, a spark hit the powder in the pan, causing the powder in the gun to explode and fire the musketball. If the hole was jammed, there was a flash, but the gun did not fire. Today a "flash in the pan" refers to someone or something that is popular for a very short while.

To go off half cocked

The **cock**, or **hammer**, of a musket was the part of the lock that flew forward and created the spark. The first step in loading a musket was

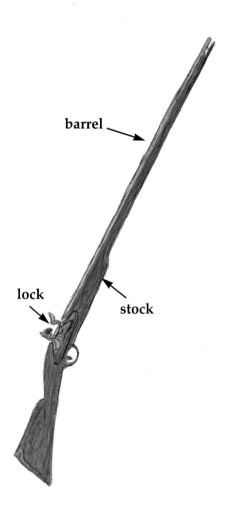

*A **musket** was a type of gun used until the 1840s. This diagram shows the musket "lock, stock, and barrel."*

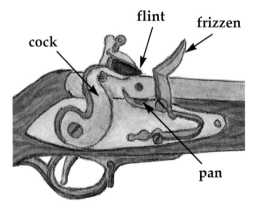

*When a musket was fired, the **cock** flew forward, hitting the **frizzen** and creating a spark.*

to pull the cock halfway back, or **half-cock** it. The last step was to fully cock the musket. If an overeager person forgot this last step, the gun would not fire. Today the phrase "to go off half cocked" refers to an attempt that fails because the proper and necessary steps were not taken to make it succeed.

Off by a long shot

Guns are not accurate when the target is far away. In settler times guns were even less accurate. A "long shot" was bound to miss the target by quite a bit. If you are "off by a long shot" at guessing the correct answer to a question, you are not close at all!

In settler times, if an arm or leg had a serious injury, such as a bullet wound, frostbite, or badly broken bone, the limb was cut off. There were no painkillers for this operation. Instead, the patient was given a bullet on which to bite so that he or she would not cry out. When someone tells you to "bite the bullet," that person wants you to accept an unpleasant situation with courage.

Early medical terms

Early medicine was like a guessing game. The settlers did not know that germs caused many diseases, so their remedies—and doctors—were often questionable.

What a quack!
When settlers were desperate for a cure, they sometimes turned to a **quacksalver**, or quack. Quacks claimed to have miracle cures for many illnesses. Some cures, however, contained dangerous and unhealthy ingredients such as opium, mercury, and alcohol. Today we sometimes call a doctor who has questionable cures a quack.

Phrenologist
The settlers believed that a **phrenologist** could understand a person's character by examining the position and size of the bumps on his or her

Catarrh was a common word used by the settlers to describe a variety of illnesses. Anyone who suffered from a sore throat, cough, shortness of breath, laryngitis, or stomach problems was thought to have catarrh. Look at the picture above. How did a patient who had catarrh feel?

head. Phrenologists claimed that the brain was divided into 40 sections, each associated with a different character trait. For example, a person with a large bump at the back of the head was said to have strong feelings.

The Doctrine of Signatures

Many doctors followed a popular theory called the **Doctrine of Signatures**. According to this theory, the shape or color of a plant held the clues or "signatures" of the illness it cured. Almonds resembled the shape of an eye, so they were eaten to improve sight. Walnuts were considered "brain" food. Can you guess why? We now know that a plant cannot cure an illness because of its shape or color!

*Many settlers suffered from a disease called **ague**. The symptoms of ague were like those of the flu. They included fever, coughing, chills, nosebleeds, and achiness. One "cure" for ague was to kill a chicken and hold its body against the patient's bare feet while he or she swallowed cobwebs that were rolled into a ball!*

Extinct expressions

Many colorful sayings that were used by the settlers are no longer in use today. You may, however, want to make them a part of your speech! Tell your parents you are "savage as a meat ax" and watch them shudder! Casually mention that you have "seen the elephant" and see if your friends roll their eyes in disbelief!

Is this woman "savage as a meat ax" or does she simply have bad manners?

Savage as a meat ax

This strange expression meant "very hungry." Sometimes an ax was used for cutting meat. If a person was "savage as a meat ax," that person was probably so hungry that his or her ferocious eating habits resembled an ax hitting meat.

Getting the mitten

If a young woman gave her boyfriend "the mitten," it was not a gift. This phrase meant that he was no longer her boyfriend. Bring this saying back to life and tell friends they will "get the mitten" if they treat you badly.

See the elephant

If someone expected something good to happen but was disappointed, he or she "saw the elephant." No one is sure about the origin of this phrase. Perhaps someone had a visit to the circus that did not meet that person's expectations.

This young boy is definitely "savage as a meat ax." He is going at his dinner "hammer and tongs!"

"Giving someone the mitten" was another way of telling a person to go away.

Seeing plain, gray, wrinkled elephants might be a letdown for some people, but if they saw these dancing elephants, they would certainly not be disappointed!

Activities and ideas

Research more sayings

Ask your parents and neighbors to tell you their favorite sayings. When you have collected ten, go to the library and research their meanings. Use different sources of information such as dictionaries and history books.

Compare the original meaning with the way the saying is used today. Share your most interesting expressions with your friends. Before you reveal the true meanings of the sayings, ask your classmates how they think the expressions originated.

Sayings with similes

When you compare one thing with another using the word "like" or "as," you have a **simile**. Sayings such as "hungry as a wolf" and "run like the wind" are similes. Match the words below to complete the similes.

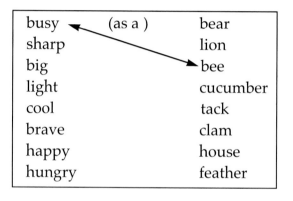

busy	(as a)	bear
sharp		lion
big		bee
light		cucumber
cool		tack
brave		clam
happy		house
hungry		feather

More fun and games!

After you have unscrambled the following sayings, make up a list of your own and ask some friends to do the same.

Don't count cats and dogs.

Water is worth two in the bush.

You can lead a horse to water over spilt milk.

Don't cry your chickens before they're hatched.

It's raining, but you cannot make him drink.

A bird in the hand under the bridge.

Each person exchanges his or her list with another player. When all the sayings are unscrambled, start again with a new batch!

Anyone for charades?

Have ten friends write one saying each on a piece of paper. Put the folded papers into a hat. Divide the group into teams and have each team draw one saying that will be acted out in front of the class. Each team now presents its saying without speaking. To begin, the first actor indicates the number of words in the saying by holding up the appropriate number of fingers. Then each team member acts out a word until the entire saying is guessed. The first team to guess the saying is the next to perform.

Figure it out!

The settlers enjoyed word puzzles. Unscramble the words in the puzzle below to reveal a popular settler saying:

utp uryo soen ot hte sordnegitn

Create puzzles using sayings from this book or ones that you have made up. Exchange puzzles with your friends.

Hold your own bee!

Now that you know what a bee is, hold your own. How about having a "sayings" bee? Divide the class into two groups. Each group chooses ten sayings from this book. Pick a team captain. He or she reads the saying aloud and uses it in a sentence. The first player in the other group must explain how that saying originated. If the answer makes sense (or is at least funny!), score one point. Then the other team takes a turn. The team that has the most points is the winner. Celebrate the fun you had with delicious treats—just as the settlers would have!

Invent your own sayings

By now you have read many common settler expressions. Why not create your own sayings? Use modern words such as the ones below to help you get started. Don't forget to write a meaning and explanation for your saying!

microwave   pasta
television   barbecue
VCR   cool
computer   boogie
rerun   sneakers
rap   bike

Create your own book

Suggest to your classmates that they, too, write some modern sayings. After compiling everyone's original expressions, have your class publish its own book of sayings. Use the school computer or your best writing. Each day, ask a different student to select a "saying-of-the-day" from the book. Then have the students write a story or poem about the saying or draw a picture to go with it. Use the saying at least three times throughout the day, and it will be your own!

Did you enjoy reading this book? We loved writing it! You, too, will have a ball writing your own "sayings" book! Many of the sayings in this book sound strange today. Imagine how odd a settler might find your modern sayings if he or she were to read your book!

Glossary

accessory A small item of dress, such as jewelry, a scarf, or a belt

artisan A skilled craftsperson

barter To bargain for a good price

bonnet A soft hat with a brim that frames the face

charades A game in which a person acts out a saying while a group tries to guess what that saying is

compile To gather information by collecting material from different sources

Conestoga wagon A large wagon with a covered top

corset A stiff, tight undergarment worn by women

flax A plant whose fibers are used to make linen

flu Also called influenza; an illness whose symptoms include coughing, fever, and headaches

forge A blacksmith's furnace

frostbite The condition of having part of one's body frozen

gunpowder An explosive mixture of chemicals

harness An arrangement of straps for attaching equipment to an animal

linen A cloth made from flax that wrinkles easily

hopper A large funnel-like bin with a small opening in the bottom for draining the contents

husk The dry outer covering of seeds or fruit

infection A disease caused by harmful germs

laryngitis An illness that causes the voice to be hoarse

liquor A strong alcoholic beverage

loom A large device used for weaving

mercury A poisonous, metallic substance

military Describing or relating to soldiers and the army

nervous system The network of nerves in people and most animals

Old English The language spoken in Britain between A.D. 700 and 1100

opium A powerful drug made from the juice of unripe poppy pods

rye A type of grain

settler A person who makes his or her home in a new country or a part of the country that is not yet developed

suspense A state of being nervous or afraid of what will happen next

textile Woven fabric

trait A special feature of someone's personality

type A small metal block with a raised character or letter that is used in printing

typeset To arrange type for printing advertisements, newspapers, or posters

values Strongly held beliefs about right and wrong

vocabulary The words spoken and used regularly by a person or a group of people

wick A thick cotton string used in making candles

yoke A wooden device worn across the neck and shoulders, used for carrying or pulling heavy loads

Index of words and phrases

Acknowledgments

Photo credits

Jim Bryant: page 17 (bottom)

Colonial Williamsburg Foundation:
pages 4-5

Marc Crabtree: pages 6, 14

Peter Crabtree: pages 8, 17 (top)

Bobbie Kalman: page 7

Black Creek Pioneer Village/TRCA: pages 9
(both), 15 (bottom), 16, 19 (both), 23

Niagara Apothecary: page 24

Illustrations & colorizations

Barb Bedell: cover

Halina Below-Spada: page 14

Andy Cienik: pages 12-13, 25, 29

Antoinette "Cookie" DeBiasi: title page,
pages 8 (both), 10 (both), 11 (both), 18, 20 (all),
21 (all), 26, 27 (all), 28, 30

Tammy Everts: pages 19, 22 (both), 23

8 9 0 Printed in U.S.A. 3 2 1